This jour

_____

I STARTED IT ON

this day: _____

in the year: _____

in the city of: _____

when I was in this grade: _____

and was _____ years old.

I COMPLETED IT ON

this day: _____

in the year: _____

in the city of: _____

when I was in this grade: _____

and was _____ years old.

IT WAS GIVEN TO ME BY:

_____

Another Keepsake Journal for Kids

More About Me

rising moon

Books for Young Readers from Northland Publishing

Other journals by Linda Kranz:

All About Me: A Keepsake Journal for Kids
Through My Eyes: A Journal for Teens
For My Child: A Mother's Keepsake Journal

These journals are available at your local bookstore
or by calling Rising Moon at 1-800-346-3257 for a
free catalog.

The text type was set in Pixie.
The cover illustration and display type were
    designed by Libba Tracy.
Composed in the United States of America.
Designed by Rudy J. Ramos, Ramos Design Studio
Edited by Stephanie Bucholz
Production Supervised by Lisa Brownfield

Printed in Selangor Darul Ehsan Malaysia April 2018

ISBN 0-87358-716-2

For my friends close by and miles away.
Thank you for your wisdom, your love,
your laughter, and the happy memories
that continually bring a smile to my face!

And for every child:
ALWAYS . . . stay young at heart
no matter how old you are!

Illustration by Kenneth J. Spengler from *A Campfire for Cowboy Billy*, written by Wendy K. Ulmer.

A Note for You

Hello again! I am so glad that you will now start your second journal. You must be very good at writing, and enjoy it; just the fact that you have *More About Me* proves it.

Or maybe you're starting with this journal. I hope you enjoy it. Once you fill up these pages, you might want to look for *All About Me* and begin your second.

Since the release of *All About Me* I have been visiting schools and speaking with students and teachers. I tell them how I got started in writing and about my journal-keeping now, and then I ask to see a show of hands: "Who in the audience is a journal writer?"

To my delight there are always a number of journal writers in the crowd and many are even using *All About Me*. Next, I ask if anyone has any questions, and hands go up all over the room:

"Will you have a second journal coming? Because I've almost finished the first journal," one student said not long ago.

"I want to keep writing. I want to be able to show my children what it was like when I was growing up," another student said.

A third student said that the questions in *All About Me* helped him "get to know a little more about the important people in his life." He, too, wanted to keep writing.

Hearing these comments truly made my day!

Also, I have received letters from students in different parts of the country who thought journal writing wasn't for them at first, but they tried it and they were hooked! Another student said, "I like the fact that this journal is for boys AND girls! So everyone can enjoy it!"

As with *All About Me,* you can skip around or go in order. You can also go back and add more to pages you've already written on: Answer a question, date it, then wait a few months and answer the question again. As you grow and experience new things, your answers may change. There are no rules. Just write!

As you fill up these pages, you are capturing your history on paper. These entries will be so interesting to look back on years from now. We all have a special story to tell. Write yours on the pages of this journal.

And a Special Note for Parents

We live in busy times. Journal writing is something you can do as a family to help you slow down and unwind. It can be a vehicle for you and your child to get to know each other better. Start by setting aside one or two nights a week: a quiet time to share these questions together.

This journal can travel on vacations in planes, trains, and cars. It can go to grandparents' houses. It can make a rainy day—or any day when a child wants "something different" to do—interesting. If you are willing to help motivate your child, these journal pages will fill up quickly.

Encourage your children to start writing now. Years from now they will thank you!

—Linda Kranz

Why are **grand-parents** special?

Ask your parents if they have a **special** *memory* about their **grand-parents**.

What is it?

If **you** could change **3** things about yourself, *what* would you **CHANGE** and why?

How would you go about **MAKING** these changes?

If I said, "The sound of **birds** singing outside *your* window early in the morning," or "The crackle of **fireworks** on a summer's night," or "The sound of a strong *wind* and *hail* hitting *your* window," what *memories* would you think of?

Write

and answer your

own question here.

Name **10**
things
that you
love ...
then keep
adding to
this list.

If you could spend an entire day—morning, afternoon, and night—being **invisible** what would you do?

What would your day be like?

If you went to visit a relative or a friend for a **week or two,** what would your family *miss most* about you?

List at least **5** things.

If you
want some
quiet time
alone, to
think,
where do
you *go?*

Why is it a
special
place?

Illustration by Jeanne Arnold from *Carlos and the Skunk/Carlos y el zorrillo*, written by Jan Romero Stevens.

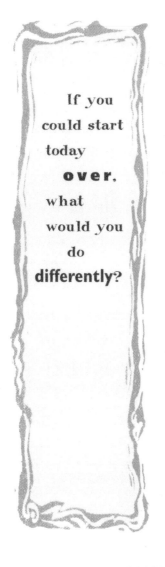

If you
could start
today
over,
what
would you
do
differently?

If you
were the
principal
of your
school, what
changes
would you
make?

What do
you think
would be the
HARDEST
part about
being a
principal?

Have you ever been **CAMPING** or to **summer camp**?

What was it like?

If you haven't, do you think you would like to *try* camping sometime?

People **communicate** in so many ways, sometimes just by a certain *look*. Can your close friends *understand* you just by the way you *look* at them?

How about your family?

What part
of the
day do
you like
the
BEST?

Why do
you look
forward
to it?

If you could **change** some family rules, what would they be?

Explain *why* you think they need to be changed.

If someone **breaks** the rules in your house, what should the punishment be?

Ask your parents how **life** has *changed* since they were **kids.**

Illustration by Libba Tracy from *It Rained on the Desert Today*, written by Ken and Debby Buchanan.

Does your family have any **traditions** that you want to carry on when you have your own family?

What are they?

How do you
help
around the
house?

Do you
pitch in
and help
or do
you have
to be
reminded?

Draw
anything you
want here.

Finish one
of these
sentences:

"Today
started
out like
any
other day,
but then..."

OR

"Lately,
more than
anything
I have
been
wishing
for..."

What *cheers* you **uP** when you are having a bad day?

How do you cheer up a friend if he or she is **sad**?

Describe a *typical* **summer** day.

What is your day like?

Name **5** of the *best* **things** that happened to you this summer.

Write about
a time
when you
did
something
that you
didn't
think you
could do.

What
was it?

How did
you **feel?**

Illustration by Lori Osiecki from *Swimming Lessons*, written by Betsy Jay.

If you could choose to live during *any* time period, would you choose to live in the **future**, the PAST, or **right now?** Explain.

Describe an occasion when you were allowed to do something for the **FIRST TIME.** What was it and how did you *feel?*

Where would you like to go on **vacation** this year? *Draw* a picture of the place here.

Describe a typical **school day.**

What is it like?

What is your **favorite** thing to do after school?

Ask your parents to think about the following question:

"What are three of your happiest memories?"

Give them a day or two to think about it and write their answer here.

What **books** have you checked out from the library this year?

Name some of your **favorites**.

PETS

have a
special
way of
making
us feel
better
when we
are *sad*
or *lonely*.

Write

about how
your pet
cheers
you up
or makes
you *laugh*.

Illustration by David Slonim from *Old Jake's Skirts*, written by C. Anne Scott.

On these **2** pages write
compliments that you have
received and who said them.

When you are feeling down,
turn to these pages and
your spirits will soar!

Does your family have a fire emergency plan? *What is it?*

Draw your route here. If your family does not have a plan, call a meeting to create one.

What is the **hardest** thing about *growing up*?

What is the **BEST** thing?

How many people do you think it is possible to **love** at one time? Explain. Name some **special** people in your life right now. Why are they important to you?

Name a few
of your
most prized
possessions
—things
that you
could
never
give away.

Why do
they
mean so
much to
you?

Draw

anything you
want here.

It's your **birthday.**

If you could plan your day, how would it **go**?

When was the last time you told your **PARENTS** that you loved them? For a change, *write a note*. Tell them why they are so special to you. They will surely treasure it. (Write those words down here, too, and add to these thoughts from time to time.)

I
wanted
to
write
THIS
down
so I
wouldn't
forget.

Write down the cost of a first class **stamp**, a gallon of **gas**, a ticket to the **movies**, the price of a **newspaper**, the cost to rent your favorite **video**. Ask your parents to help you with other items your family buys. It will be interesting to see how prices have changed when you are **older**.

Everyone has habits. Some are good and some are bad. Name some of your **good** and **bad** habits.

Ask your parents how they chose your **name**— the story behind it.

What other names did they consider?

Do you have a **nickname**?

How did you get it?

Has anyone ever **embarrassed** you?

What happened?

How did you get over it?

Have you ever had a
substitute teacher?

How did your day go?
What do you think it would be
like to come into a classroom
that you have never been to
before, and teach for
a day or two?

Illustration by Libba Tracy from *Building a Bridge* written by Lisa Shook Begaye

If a **NEW** student came into your class after the school year had started, how would you make him or her feel **welcome?**

What's
different
about this
school
year
compared to
last year?

Write
about how
school has
changed
for you
now that
you are a
year **older**.

Write

and answer your
own question here.

If you
could choose
anyone to
be your
best friend,
who would
you pick?

Why?

How many
CLOSE
friends do
you have?

*Who are
they?*

What makes
your
friendship
with them
strong?

What do
you like
best about
your
family?

How is
your family
different
from some of
your friends'
families?

How is it
the **same**?

Have you ever felt *sorry* for someone?

Why?

What happened?

When you
are grown
and have
a home of
your own,
what will
you do
that
you aren't
allowed to
do now?

Write down
a favorite
family recipe
or two on
this page.

People are always inventing
NEW PRODUCTS. What would
you like to invent?
Draw it here.

Be honest. If you make a mess, clean it up. Be a good listener. Be honest.

Be a good listener. Be honest. If you make a mess, clean it up. Be a good listener. Be honest.

Be honest. If you make a mess, clean it up. Be a good listener. Be honest. If you make a mess, clean

it up. Be a good listener. If you make a mess, clean it up.

Do you
play any
**team
sports**?

What do
you *like*
about it?

If you don't
play a
sport, how
do you
spend your
**free
time**?

Kids often **tease** one another. Have you ever been teased?

About what?

How did you *feel*?

How did you **get over** it?

Illustration by Lori Osiecki from *Swimming Lessons*, by Betsy Jay.

Name **3** things you could do to show you are a **good** friend. Keep adding to this list.

Do you remember the most colorful
sunset that you have ever seen?
Draw it here.

Describe your favorite **smell**, *color*, and **sound**.

Why do you like them so much?

What do they **remind** you of?

Write
and answer your
own question here.

How do you
feel when
someone
shares
something
with you?

Do you find
it easy
to share?

Name some
examples
of how
you have
shared.

The best
thing that
happened
to me
today
was . . .

The best
thing that
happened
to me **this
week**
was . . .

Write about a few of the worst things you **EVER** remember tasting.

Then write about some of your *favorite* things to eat.

Illustration by Jim Harris from *Jack and the Giant: A Story Full of Beans*, written by Jim Harris.

Suppose you are working on a **project**, and no matter what you do, it won't work out right. Would you keep *trying*, take a break and try again **later**, ask an older sister or brother or your parents for **help**, or give up?

Explain.

How do you
**get
along**
with your
brothers
and sisters?

Or, if
you are an
only child,
write about
how you
and your
friends
get along.

Which season is your favorite: **winter,** *spring,* **summer,** or **fall**?

Why do you like it so much?

Why is it important to write a *thank-you* letter after you receive a gift?

How long does it take you to reply?

Would you always want to be the age you are right *now*?

Why or why not?

When you get together with friends, do you like to go to **their** houses or stay at **your house**?

Why?

What do you do when you get together?

Have you
ever grown
something
from a
seed?

Did you
eat
what
you grew?

How did
it *taste*?

Illustration by Robert Chapman from *A Gift for Abuelita: Celebrating the Day of the Dead/Un regalo para Abuelita: En celebración del Día de los Muertos*, written by Nancy Luenn.

Which
takes more
courage—
to tell the
truth
or to tell
a *lie*?

Why do
you feel
this way?

Is there
something
that you
have been
wanting
to learn
but for
some reason
it hasn't
happened
yet?

What is it?

How can
you make
sure it
will
happen?

How do you and your family spend your time during **winter break and** *spring break?*

What do you do?

Draw

anything you

want here.

Keep a box in your room for your special
treasures. Years from now it will be fun
to look back and see what was *important*
to you when you were younger. Draw a
picture of the items in the box here.
Write what they are next to the drawings.

Ask your parents how they *felt* the first time they **saw you**.

What are their *memories* of that day?

Have you ever saved up your **money** to buy something *special?*

What was it?

Or are you saving for some thing right now?

What is it?

Illustration by Jeanne Arnold from *Carlos and the Cornfield/Carlos y la milpa de maíz,* written by Jan Romero Stevens.

Ask your parents these questions:

"If you could choose any job, what would it be?"

"What *advice* would you give me about deciding on a **career?**"

Write about their answers.

If you could plan your **perfect** day, what would it be like?

Write

and answer your
own question here.

Can you tell by looking at someone if they are **friendly** or **smart**, or whether they have the same interests as you?

Explain.

How would you find out what they were like?

How long does it take you to get to know someone?

Are you
a good
listener?

Do you let
your
friends and
family
finish a
sentence, or
do you jump
in and talk
before
they have
finished?

Explain.

What do/did your grandparents do for a living?

Ask your parents what they remember about their parents' jobs when they were growing up.

Write

and answer your

own question here.

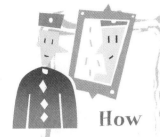

How would you **describe** yourself to someone who didn't know you?

Write not only about how you *look* but also about your **likes** and **dislikes**.

How do you **participate** in class?

Do you raise your hand often?

Do you offer to help other students when they don't understand an assignment?

Explain.

Everyone has an **im-agina-tion.**

What do *you* like to imagine?

What are
some of the
**funniest
things**
that have
ever
happened
to you?

Describe
a time
when you
couldn't
stop
laughing.

Illustration by Libba Tracy from *Building a Bridge*, written by Lisa Shook Begaye.

CLOUDS can be fascinating.
So many **shapes**.

Go outside on a cloudy day and
look for pictures in the clouds.

Draw some of them here.

When something is **troubling** *you,* **write it down.**

Then, next to your concerns, write down some **positive** things that could happen instead of only the **negative** things.

When you are out riding around on your **bike**, either doing errands or on your way to and from school, take time to **notice** something that you *haven't* seen before in your own **neighborhood** or **city**.

Write about it.

Illustration by Kenneth J. Spengler from *A Campfire for Cowboy Billy*, written by Wendy K. Ulmer.

Do you *remember* a *time* when you wanted a special item for a **long time** and then received it as a 𝓰𝓲𝓯𝓽?

What was it?

And was it **everything** that you *imagined* it would be?

Do you consider yourself a little shy, very shy, or not shy at all?

Explain.

Write

and answer your
own question here.

Have you ever seen a falling star?

Draw a picture of it here.

If you haven't seen a falling star,
draw what you think one would look like.

Have your
parents ever
surprised
you?

Like *writing*
you a note
and putting
it in your
lunch box?

Or picking
you up
from school
so you
wouldn't
have to
walk in bad
weather?

Can you
think
of any
surprises?

What is your regular **bedtime** on school nights?

On the **weekend?**

Do you fall asleep by reading, listening to music, or something else?

Make a
list of
things you
want to
do when
you get
older.
Keep
adding
to this
list.

What do you *bring* to school for **lunch** every day, or what do you **buy** for lunch?

What do
you think
about
sleepovers?

Have you
ever had
any
sleepovers
at your
house?

Why are
they **fun**?

Write
about
some of
your
favorite
sleepover
memories.

Compared to last year, do you have **more** or **less** homework this school year?

What are your study habits?

What
is the
scariest
dream
you
remember?
Describe it.

Your
happiest
dream?
Describe it.

Illustration by James Bernardin from *Dancing with the Wind*, written by Stanton Orser.

Do you remember
the most colorful **rainbow**
you have ever seen?

Draw a picture of it here.

Have you
ever gotten
upset
with your
parents and
said things
that you
shouldn't
have said?

*What
happened?*

Did you
talk it
over?

Did either
of you
say you
were
sorry?

Draw

anything you

want here.

Parents *teach* us many things as we grow up. Can you name some things that *you* would like to teach *your* parents?

IDEAS for when you have nothing to do:

Ask your parents if you can look at a family **photo album**.

Read a NEW book or reread one of *your favorites*.

Play with a pet. You will both get some exercise.

Make crafts to **give** to friends or relatives.

Draw or paint with **watercolors**.

Write a letter to a **friend** or **relative**.

Clean out your closet or drawers: You might find **special treasures** that you thought were lost.

Offer to HELP your parents with household chores. That will give them more time to relax and more time to **spend** with you.

Use the next few lines to write in your own ideas. Then, when you have extra time on your hands, you can turn to this page in your journal and you will have many ideas to choose from that will keep you busy.

LINDA KRANZ began writing as a teenager. A locking diary given to her on her thirteenth birthday was the vehicle that encouraged her to take to the page. Growing up in a military family and moving around a lot gave Linda plenty to write about.

Later, she passed her fondness for journaling on to her daughter, whose interest in keeping her own journal inspired Linda to write *All About Me: A Keepsake Journal for Kids*, also from Northland Publishing.

Linda lives with her husband, Klaus, daughter Jessica, and son Nikolaus in the mountains of Flagstaff, Arizona.

The author would enjoy hearing from you about your thoughts on journal writing and any suggestions you may have for future journals. Write to:

Linda Kranz
c/o Rising Moon
P.O. Box 1389
Flagstaff, AZ 86002-1389